PRAISE
Shift

Why do I love these poems? There's so much: expressions of vulnerability that are only the products of courage since every revelation (for the reader) seems powerful by the moment, "earned" as they say—this is no mere stylist, but someone who can turn the camera to the violent, sensual and passionate by turns. There's a great deal of formal constraint, elegance and mastery, and shout-outs to predecessors to whom he has apprenticed, only there to advertise the bounds he, himself, has broken. Counter to the tyranny of the social media Blitzkreig, James's poems are filled with acts of *attention* that, in a way, are what I am most envious of—he's taken the ephemeral, intense, and perhaps better-left-forgotten, moments of anxiety, love, eroticism, the strictures of the family, the wilds of momentary encounters when aesthetics and lust mix ("You'd have made me do anything with /your Sal Mineo-James Dean wattage"), the bumping up of the individual with the city, largely Los Angeles, itself ("Beyond our fly-spattered / windshield soft-lit brides and grooms / wave along the i-95") and let them find their way into his poetry. But for all of his focus on the body and desire, situation and society, language thrives: "At MacArthur Park, kobicha and svelte, / Derek walked in and out the frame / befitting the stomach's swell. / He omm'd himself silly in the echo / of the underpass ever after." Regardless of where James is "going" with his poetry—I think it will be far, this is an awesome first step—read this modest set and relearn to live.

BRIAN KIM STEFANS
author of *"Viva Miscegenation": New Writing* and many other books

Emily Dickenson's slant vision informs Randy James' Coltrane-like improvised and formalized poetry. James' oblique, roundabout, taciturn sensibility insists on individual complexity against groupthink, unless that group seeks justice.

The shift of the title suggests a process, something being made, that which is against fixity. Fluidity is the order of the day, and poetry is the republic for this mutable citizenry, this insistence on the protean body and the ethical community, no straightjackets, no more limiting behavioral ethos, just a free and childlike body feeling its way and naturally inclined towards Whitmanesque, all-in, comprehensive and multitudinous joy.

There's no more sophisticated a dance than this pivot between self and community and the beauty of the two working in harmony to become a threesome.

As his mother says,

> "It's good to have fruits in the house.
> You have fruit then you not poor."

The poet benefits from this sustenance and offers readers and listeners his fruitful imaginary as supplement, canticle, song and dance.

FRED D'AGUIAR
author of *Continental Shelf*

Randy James brings nerve and nuance to a handbook of poetic forms: abecedarian, bop, pantoum, ghazal, ode, ekphrastic and concrete poems—writes of passage for a tough and tender son, brother, lover on a journey to happily-ever-after with stops in Clubland on the way to a Vegas wedding chapel. "Where shall I take my Bride?/ I will take him where metalwork points all directions."

HARRYETTE MULLEN
author of *Urban Tumbleweed: Notes from a Tanka Diary*

"I am invisible," the poet tells us of his childhood. "I am thought an afterthought." But that was then; these poems are Now. In *Shifters*, Randy James explodes into visible power, an explorer of form, a magician of image. These are poems of Black queer man-ifestation, of maturing, of naming. James's lyrics are packed with action and object: road trips and voguing, fireworks and an eighth of mushrooms, blood and spit. Desire is fuel, language is combustion, and James blazes across these moonlit pages like a charioteer. He puts form to feeling and makes you see what you didn't know was right there all along.

K. M. SOEHNLEIN
author of *The World of Normal Boys* and
You Can Say You Knew Me When

Don't be fooled by the size of this "little" book of poems by Randy James. They are enormous in scope and as packed with the pleasures of language—and why else read poetry?—as much more published writers. If this is the beginning of his career I'd say he's been remarkably circumspect about publishing. Here he explores deftly compressed poems addressing race, gender, eroticism, origin myth, and attachment.

Poems trace the poet's complicated selves in remarkably nimble language packed with surprising implication. There is "a sky of blasted chrysanthemums," a person with "a trampoline smile," someone whose "flip flops land like medicine balls," and he notes "constellated fireflies fail in Morse code." Yet like every lyric poet worth the name, he writes eloquently on death, including "Le petit mort" where "you ferry the self, / make the body/ un caisson for release." In "Deliriant," the angel's "milli-feathers beat the air/ shooing what's alive/from the center of my eyes" although the erotic charge is never far from death—he writes of "my right hand lipping/Azrael's flowers – the devil's trumpet." More than living up to the book's title, *Shifters*, the brilliant movement of subject and language make you want to hear a lot more from this poet—and SOON.

KAREN KEVORKIAN
author of *Quivira, Lizard Dream,* and *White Stucco Black Wing*

Shifters

Randy James

NOMADIC PRESS

OAKLAND

111 FAIRMOUNT AVENUE
OAKLAND, CA 94611

BROOKLYN

475 KENT AVENUE #302
BROOKLYN, NY 11249

WWW.NOMADICPRESS.ORG

MASTHEAD

FOUNDING AND MANAGING EDITOR
J. K. FOWLER

ASSOCIATE EDITOR
MICHAELA MULLIN

EDITOR
JAMES CAGNEY

MISSION STATEMENT

Nomadic Press is a 501 (C)(3) not-for-profit organization that supports the works of emerging and established writers and artists. Through publications (including translations) and performances, Nomadic Press aims to build community among artists and across disciplines.

SUBMISSIONS

Nomadic Press wholeheartedly accepts unsolicited book manuscripts. To submit your work, please visit www.nomadicpress.org/submissions

DISTRIBUTION

Orders by trade bookstores and wholesalers:
Small Press Distribution,
1341 Seventh Street
Berkeley, CA 94701
spd@spdbooks.org
(510) 524-1668 / (800) 869-7553

Shifters

© 2021 by Randy James

This book was made possible by a loving community of chosen family and friends, old and new.

For author questions or to book a reading at your bookstore, university/school, or alternative establishment, please send an email to info@nomadicpress.org.

Cover artwork and author portrait by Arthur Johnstone

Published by Nomadic Press, 111 Fairmount Avenue, Oakland, CA 94611

First printing, 2021

LIBRARY OF CONGRESS CATALOGING-IN-PUBLICATION DATA

Randy James 1984 –
Title: *Shifters*
P. CM.
Summary: Part memorial, part snapshot, part fancy, *Shifters* is a testament to the self and the act of seeing. A meditation on Blackness and queerness under duress, *Shifters* reacts to the power of the moment and finds joy in the power of the actor and the witness.

[1. POETRY. 2. BLACKNESS. 3. LGBTQIA+. 4. AMERICAN GENERAL.] I. III. TITLE.

LIBRARY OF CONGRESS CONTROL NUMBER: 2021932308

ISBN: 978-1-7363963-9-1

Shifters

Randy James

**NOMADIC
PRESS**

CONTENTS

CLASSROOM GUIDE

INTRODUCTION

A lot of writers, or at least I believe, will tell you there was no other choice. There's a necessity to committing words and phrases to the page because life dictates it that way. This book is born from that necessity.

I started writing this book ten years ago, under a different title. Most of the poems from that first iteration have not made it to this book, but the need to "get it down on paper" persisted through all of its versions. But first, I had to find the right language. To find the right language, I needed to live my life.

These poems thrive on the tension between reality and expectation. A 4th of July gone awry, the passing of friends in the prime of life, theft on a night out in a big city—these are curveballs that have the power to change the direction of a life. It's not all haphazard, however. There's joy here, too—the prospect of new love, a monumental museum exhibit, dancefloor abandon.

It's the act of witnessing! This collection is a testament to the power of witnessing and naming. In reading *Shifters*, I hope that you are activated by your own capacity to witness the shifting parameters of life; to heed the call of seeing, yourself and others, more fully.

PLACEMENTS

Aggressive men live on the reverse end of my table. Indeed,
before hair grew in new places, before their square jawlines, our
chairs took far ends of the long wood. My
dreams end with a remove from the locker room.

Essentialism argues my selves be kept within a
frame dictated by my color relative to Mother Earth. How
girded the heart must be to withstand a man's open smile, or
his pouty lips, his toss of a napkin. I am

invisible; mass between table and chair. Their chuckling is a
jail, their brother-words sharp with exclusion. They say,
"Kill. Kill the difference blooming from a lisp &
limp wrist. Kill the secret of possessing joy. We barred any & all

matrons. There is no refuge or respite here with us, boy.
Never a man." I am made nervous, keep my head bent,
obsequious. Secretly, I sway from canticles in the drag of *basso
profundo*. In this pressing dinner arrangement,

quagmire abides in the valley of the shadow of dinner plates &
reservations. I stare at placements, lost among forks for salad or fruit.
Sweat floods the trenches of my fingerprints. Our image in cutlery,
traitorous. I have not lifted my head. I locate in the

unbent pitch of virile voices, crumbs caught in moustaches. Our
verity lives in lapels, under china and the flirt of shined shoes—but this
whispering is nearly half-done. For the rest, I will lean into these
xeric conditions, mistake ambience for ultraviolet rays, assume

yawping is the work of revival. I will not leave my place until
zero hour, when all-aggression returns to The Alpha & Omega.

MY FAMILY / REMAINS

My brother taught me how to walk—there's
a Polaroid as evidence,
and by channeling God
I could read early, speak on R-Rated realities,
like the yes! flung from my two-year mouth
as we flew from daddy to Mamá's.

Almost impossible to do
Reciting the makings of you

I don't know the origin story,
what a seminary girl from Rio Abajo saw
in a soldier boy from 'Bama sticks. I know the fruit
of their first conception is a prophesied diamond,
and I am the fruit come after, twinkle
in the wake of his fated trail. The way my
mother tells it, God gave the OK to have me, but
to my child-ear, I am thought an afterthought.

Almost impossible to do
Reciting the makings of you

That's a lie. I see mama's fall in a picture of papa. In it,
he is in a barber's throne sporting an immaculate afro,
prominent eyes, easy smile. Daddy fell for the wine in momma's
akimbo stance – I have seen that photo, too. In turn,
I am the final evidence: a silver-born
babe at play in Earth's cradle.

CHARM & STRANGE & SATELLITE

Camping ends without hitch. Supplies secure
in your sun-beaten trunk, we leave Portola

Redwoods for home. As the I-5 sluices
through my right-hand in La Honda,

we enact an inverted *Driving Miss Daisy.*
I watch your discerning hand direct course,

from Portola to Frisco, in the glow
of Independence. Forgive me, I rammed

this Corolla E80 into your
neighbor's boat propeller and offered nothing.

One red night, I spy your moony eyes
in the bright lights of Gerald Desmond.

I seize the dial and, in the a.m.
of this carpool you turn and say, bleary-eyed,

"I will destroy you." On the ride's cool end,
we sing *The White Album* from "U.S.S.R."

to "Goodnight," our whine without bristle
our goodbye in the pull up to my drive.

Cl ub

After checking, I notice the iPod missing from my coat pocket. I step onto the floor with no ballroom pedigree, leave with little fanfare. "When a queen is a non-event, *that*, children, is what we call tragedy." Our bracelets & boas bespeak Black magic, our magic shablams on Father Time.

I step onto the floor with no ballroom pedigree, leave with little fanfare. "Minorities do not fit into the gentrification plans of the city." Our bracelets & boas bespeak Black magic, our magic shablams on Father Time. The girls lip synch to a T *y todo* – will cut you if you act funny.

"Minorities do not fit into the gentrification plans of the city." Slinky in thongs, Long Islands in hand, the go-go boys are kinetic. The girls lip synch to a T *y todo* – will cut you if you act funny. That front on the train is façade; I know a you that lives in the lens of a Nikon.

Slinky in thongs, Long Islands in hand, the go-go boys are kinetic. A queen reveals his blowout, windmilling the inches. That front on the train is façade, I know a you that lives in the lens of a Nikon. Classics turn the houses out, feeling cunt's *raison d'etre*.

After checking, I notice the iPod missing from my coat pocket.

La nd

SHOULDERS

Some men love each other by reflection. Last night
on the bus, I saw one rest his head on another's shoulder.
Yes, Archie and Jughead snuggled, clasped hands.
The other men show their dissent with stiff shoulders.
Yet, silence. The lovers continue their oblivious occupation.
Stops come and go, there's caution at the soft shoulder,
rolling over alligator asphalt, there's caution at the potholes.
The axles keeps balance with Jughead's hand on Archie's shoulder.
Of the two, Archie's stop is first, their goodbye unceremonious.
Jughead departs soon thereafter. I give angle-eyes the cold shoulder.

TONIGHT CALLS FOR A POULTICE

Ladyfingers lit
like a birthday candle
discover nerves
beneath a fingernail,
affix, erupt.

Voice and blood conjoin
under a sky of blasted
chrysanthemums.

Hand is kept agonizingly
alive by flare, ache.

Bowels birth a dread
you can rub between
your thumb and index
as sparklers dance
away abandon.

Medic lights revolve
as an EMT compresses.

As they fade down the block,
quarter sticks rattle windows,
send car alarms singing.

DIM LIGHT / THANKSGIVING 2007

I take his length with aplomb,
watch him reach to lips and tongue
aside this Mission Revival home.

Control wrought from kneeling—
I work for the bungee in his eyes.

His completion is a sweetness
I spit to the ground.

After, he asks
if I am okay, almost
caresses my cheek,
the bungee replaced
by an abyss.

Looking up as air
seeps into us,
I smile, stranger
with each inhalation.

ODE TO A GODFLOWER

Le petit mort—
relief from the quotidian—
you ferry the self,
Make the body
un caisson for release.

Le petit mort—
I relish your
pleasure paradox
with deference.

Do you feel
the fight in our limbs
as I slip and dive
into your little deaths?

Yes, your name runs
short in English,
made a dirty thing.

Blame the Puritans.
True believers
don't blame you
for the lame
around your name.

Le petit mort,
you are the allotted
piece of God—
the exhaling O
and pursing clench,

the flight from fight,

the rib and ribbed.

DELIRIANT
AFTER E.E. CUMMINGS

Azrael descends from the heavens—decrees, *Time has run out.*
> He withers the flowers.
> To his four faces belong four mouths.
> His milli-feathers beat the air,
> shooing what's alive
>> from the center of my eyes.

Azrael offers darkness
> as compress for the restless body—
> thwarts poppy-dreams in winged mastery.
>> But, in the moment I am made to drown with his other sea-girls,
>> I surface. His mystery

>> sustained, I wear my flesh
>>> again, rise
>>> into the domino of woozy years,

>> my right-hand lipping
Azrael's flowers—
>> the devil's trumpet—by the light of the moon.

I CARRY HER WATER FROM THE WELL

I throw a pick against the body of my acoustic guitar &
    from the living room, her antennae pick up the infraction. Compelled
  by her alien anger, I come to the cross in her eyes, the unnamed
    creeping to my extremities.
She asks & asks & the root of the unsaid swells
to a three-letter crest & awash, I spill. She is made to know.
      She is made incredulous. Her lips form perfect disgust.
"I will stop believing if He doesn't change this,"
  says the woman who floods each night with cries
   to Him unseen. & now, a three-letter word
  clings to her son, another cry
    to utter, "Come. We are going to fix this."
We fall into the lived-in chocolate ottoman
   for the test of faith. She prays from a place
  where voice assumes a tidal force. Her whoa,
     it ebbs from my fifteen-year-old heart.
I pray to presuppose a miracle.
  She plays hype man. In the span
     of a fraction, I pull the bucket up.
    Her water jostles beyond the pail.

SUM / DAZE ON A HILL

Instead of descent in a lift full of penises that flaunt their boys, you find a sealed Band-Aid at the end of seven flights you first mistook for a fire escape. In the lobby, Celine—almost always offering while others back away—steps into the middle of the path. With a mauve lip she says, "Today has been a day," and all the other closer eyes break their formation, but not her & her trampoline smile. Your shoulders respond like a minute hand descending more stairs where pairs of legs travel in threes and flip flops land like medicine balls. Poetry is offensive, you think, imagining a poached horn on your chest as you charge through the dining hall. You make yourself a work of art every night you dine alone. You eat upon a tightrope, and the next day is Richard with the violent last name and puckish hazel eyes. His fine fingers, like a bird or baby, reach for the air in and out his pockets, rest on his lips, and somewhere in the middle of the day, the sun starts to slouch. You apply too much grapefruit lip balm, and so your finger is forced to do the work of a failed first application. Later that night, you take a call from a strong ellipsis who tells you he's now living in Nebraska. You think, *a Thoreau moment*, and imagine the shared laughter from such a give of pretense.

SHIFTERS

In Los Angeles,
you watch light
scale a sign. The shine
is sweet and aches
the eye. You forgot
to wear shades but
you don't own any.
The last person
with a pair couldn't
wait to cross white lines
distancing you from him.
Y'all unequally yoked,
the woman at Coast
Barber Shop might say.

In Philadelphia
at the golden hour,
you frame factories
in an Instagram story
that will vanish by Sunday.
Though it is now Monday,
the tale it told
will live through loop
of digital ether.

In Detroit,
you whistle-melodize
to her clacking barrettes.
The girl asks with her eyes
what you, wordless, sing.
You smile at the meet
of absent minds.

INSTAURATION

Jordan taps my shoulder
saves me from appraising
people as effluvium

We cannot help but show
how in time we are
how we are flowers
with no one
on receiver's end

Jordan asks after my spirit
as the static of strange
voices twitch his lips

I think of God
and my answer to Jordan evades

We are unsafe on Bruin Walk

Still, Jordan extends
his thumb-ringed hand

In quarter hugs
we make each other men

DIAPHANOUS
FOR DEREK FORD

I.

She is not what I expect—dressed
as if she forgot the day. She approaches
the dais, the Mother-Nurse
of Derek Ford's final days.

The terse underline she draws
by leaving it in Jesus' hands
fills the saints, but the rest
his favorite ex-lover fills in, telling us
D's favorite word was diaphanous.

II.

Alvarado St. does not waver.
His bachelor pad residing over
MacArthur Park—where
my t-shift self-collapsed
and Hebrew flashed the walls
—does not waver either.

All the piss I learned could relieve
my athlete's foot, all the rose
oil spritzes and mistaking Kemet,
the loop of I*n a Beautiful Place
Out in the Country*—they waver not.

III.

Once upon a summertime
we ate an eighth of mushrooms,
bared our bellies in makeshift midriffs
and took an Alvarado promenade.

In Ross Dress for Less,
we, taller and darker
than the Indios in the aisles,
became *chocolate y café*.

At MacArthur Park, kobicha and svelte,
Derek walked in and out the frame
befitting the stomach's swell.
He om'd himself silly in the echo
of the underpass ever after.

JOELLE (5 TO 7)
FOR JOELLE ANTONIO MERCEDES

Joelle is a French tulip
        a Cock's Comb a Painter's-palette
Joelle is a Bird of Paradise

He claims humpbacks as ancestors
as he breaststrokes on Houston Street

and flash of green, he spurts
 ahead in a crown of laughter,
chucks a glance back

Lithe of step, he fills each second to the brim

In SoHo, on Broadway,
 we frolic in the waning day
and the austere shadows
 as storefronts mirror the sidewalk bustle
a pigeon beats against its reflection

We are captured candidly on Spring Street
 by a Dutch tourist who thanks us,
never to be seen again

Later, on a Bushwick stoop, we take a selfie
 with the lighting subdued

In it, we tilt our heads together
 like sunflowers in the rain

I WOKE UP SAME TIME HE DIED

At the service,
an Airman finely passes
the American flag to us

It compliments
his dim golden urn

My brother is at the lectern
I cry, carry on, unsightly

Mama's not, though
she never divorced him

When they lived together,
Daddy threatened her
demise by math
of rifle and backyard, called her
ugly with his pressing heel

So hard,
Mama prayed over
her second child's fate
Tells me Father
God gave the OK

At the lectern, my brother named
for the singer of three little birds,
hums with eyes wet and bright

He held the body's hand, says
Pop knew and requested

the blinds parted

Oblivious - the Carob leaves
Oblivious - the Autumnal Equinox

When I saw what my father left,
I sang "Pale September,"
holding his hardened hand,
his body blood dry

In my absence, his body
grew a side door, ate itself
an exit

SUEDE INTERIORS

It's good to have fruits in the house.
You have fruit then you not poor.

With an island lilt, my mother
wipes dust from her home's
never-wilting flora.

I store away the grocer's plastic,
rip & trash the hole-y bags.
The rice taps, filling its container
as a neighbor's car idles.

Driver outside
coughs a long time.
"Choosey Lover" mingles
with Easter's BBQ.

From their porch:

I love you. Be careful. Don't forget
them cigarettes.

                    You know I won't.

Driver&friend leave
to a saxophone speech,
Mr. Gaye radiating,
blessing the chassis.

Smoke & Arabic numbers
& Kelly Blue Book say
Silver – 2nd place –
is the best car color to buy, but

them burgundy
        interiors & car phones,
            Altima sunroofs &
                Denker skies, them
                    revving Mazda Rx-7's,
                        them woofers—
                            them hopeful fruits
                                beg to differ

FOURTH OF JULY, FIVE YEARS
FOR HAYAT HYATT

At Williamsburg Bridge—
      the steel trusses and sighing
      streetlamps the going steady
      in twined orbit—
who initiated our hands?

Two Black boys in reflective
judgment, in the climb
of an Obamaian summer
with no need for sweaters
or long pants—

and you, in that photo—
cross-legged
before a chalky
render of the City we discovered
at the bridge-mouth—

                I continue to look for it,
             hope it will be
                  found, or hope
             you tell me
                   where it is

A MARRIAGE IN TWO MOVEMENTS

I.

The Bride folds without blinders
         keeps a promise by holding hands

Their shoes - hers and the groom's -
         flatten autumn grass
as they inch around the sculpture garden

An incidental audience
sometimes laughs
         says *like* a lot

They reach a patch
of sunlight and she smiles
 without lifting her lids
  without letting go

Her ring finger kisses
 the folds in his palm

Their free hands
 caress the modern shapes

II.

Where shall I take my Bridegroom?

I will take him where metalwork
points all directions, take his hand

with my steady arm, lead him
away from strange laughter

He will smile from the tactile
His brow will furrow, figuring my fingers

We will ease
into breathing loss
of orientation
in the sculpture garden.

A DUMMY'S VENT

I chatter when he puts his hand
under my shirt
and rolls my eyes, opens my mouth
It makes them laugh
The lights make him sweat
His palm soaks the fabric
of my shirt it smells
when he forgets to do the laundry

Once, a guy with a great gap
between his teeth gave us
the chance to make
our biggest audience laugh,
but we blew it

I could not speak
in time with his words
as he kept my eyes closed
Our shirts dripped

When it was over,
the silent crowd clapped,
the host rushed a thanks
as stage lights dimmed

All that's left now
are old folks' homes,
kids' parties,
empty glasses
and half-empty bars

I tag along
I don't say much
I don't mind
I only wish he'd do the laundry more often

WHY I WRITE POETRY
AFTER MAJOR JACKSON

Because I ran away from dance on the first day

Because the Johnsons and their *ValueTales*
    Because Tikki Tikki Tembo-no Sa Rembo-chari
       Bari Ruchi-pip Peri Pembo
Because the broken-winged bird in Langston's "Dreams"

    Because of Shel Silverstein
       zils glossolalia and tambourines

Because a hard father full of feeling
       told me words are where people joked
         they could hide the world from us

Because in the 7th grade I was the only boy on fire
    in the bathroom after volleyball practice
Because in the 8th grade I made myself laugh at nothing
      'til my stomach buckled

Because of how the clarinet and chamberlain sound
Because that floating plastic bag entered and never left

Because I am melancholic
 Because it is chameleon
    Because it would be impractical
        to cry in response
       to every worthy thing
        throughout the day

Because I like opening the door
                      to let in the spirit
Because I am not a preacher nor a jazz musician

Because conflict equals response   and poems are bits of both

Because love shows itself best
      in the afterword

ROMEO & RIFF

You fight your father
in the middle of the street
and none of the neighbors make a peep

Father and son sauced
bloodletting like sailors
copping their moxie

Your navy cardigan resilient
your dad's dingy white tee
the stuff of working men's lore

What night music—beleaguered
breath braiding through scuffle

Reaching home, I cry to Coldplay
on my bathroom's tile floor
tears to "Daylight" in the full moon dark

Truth is, if you were built to like boys
I would know real trouble

You can make me do anything
with your Sal Mineo-James Dean wattage
dimples and cigarettes
You are my first Salvation
Army my first hotbox

We are Portishead in half-morning light
Everclear with Sloppy Meateaters

You are the pre-chorus in The Strokes' "Hard to Explain"

One night in the San Rafael Hills
you sang "For No One" to the skyline

What a jerk Paul McCartney is to not keep
his talent hidden to prevent dashing boys
from their best Clooney-at-karaoke impressions
Lines of boys who can't help treating
things around them like piffle

You wear Macca's coat of arms,
Romeo, and you are forgiven

MÁQUINA DE ESCRIBIR LUNAR (LUNAR TYPEWRITER)
AFTER LEANDRO KATZ

                                    for night sky—
Look what I have given up
                        Shift and Escape. Exclamation mark. Zero. Look
        what I have retained: Tabular
                            —with a press, I erect columns
                        that hold my phases of the moon,
                                my exquisite lunar syntax.
MAR(gin) REL(ease)

                    I have kept ampersand.
                            Comma colon period and question,
                                for sure footing. The dash—

for breath. Yet,

                                        I
                                      have
                                     traded
                                     chains
                                    of letter
                                    for moon
                                    sentences,
                                     moon lists,
                                      and moon
                                            poems—

                        composed full love
                     notes by that tenor
                    of night light.

My alphabet is stuff of astrologers, astronomers, and selenographers.
Like them, my typewriter follows that orb of night—Earth's first satellite.

PICTURES PRONE TO ELOPEMENT

Beyond our fly-spattered windshield
soft-lit brides and grooms
wave along the I-95

Attire soiled from leavings tangle in our headlights

Night sky and roadside keep
our eyes on altar-ephemera

Horses sail past spouses trail
exhaust in contemporania

The embers of our engine
like constellated fireflies fail
in Morse code

We bypass the turnoff to chapel   Though legal now
we choose to speed   on gelignite dreams

CLASSROOM GUIDE

A shifter is described by Oxford Languages as a person or thing that shifts something. It is also defined, in the North American context, as a gearbox of a motor vehicle or a set of gear levers on a bicycle. Both meanings involve movement. Considering these definitions, how is movement, figuratively or literally, illustrated in *Shifters*?

What are some of the ways that masculinity shifts how we see ourselves? What are some of the ways that masculinity shifts how we see others? Is there an opposite term for toxic masculinity? If so, what is it?

Our friends are often where we come to define ourselves apart from our families. But family can also be our best friends. Our friends can also be our family. How do you define friends? How do you define family?

In the face of the world's injustices, how do you find moments of joy?

What have been some moments in your life that you'd define as shifters?

PROMPTS

1. Write a poem in response to a poem in *Shifters*.

2. An abecedarian is a poem in which the first letter of each line or stanza follows sequentially through the alphabet. "Placements" is a poem that utilizes this form to explore masculinity and belonging in the speaker's effort to define himself for himself. Using the abecedarian, compose a poem about gender roles and/or belonging that defines yourself for yourself.

3. The Bop is a recent invention by poet Afaa Michael Weaver devised during a retreat at Cave Canem. It consists of three stanzas (6-8-6),

each followed by a repeated line, or refrain, that takes on a different purpose in the overall argument of the poem.

The first stanza states the problem, the second stanza explores the problem. The third stanza find resolution to the problem. If a solution cannot be found, the third stanza stands testament to that failure.

"My Family / Remains" is a Bop that examines the speaker's family's dynamic. Try your hand at a Bop. Write about anything you like, so long as it follows the Bop structure.

4. A pantoum is a poem of any length, composed of four-line stanzas in which the second and fourth lines of each stanza serve as the first and third lines of the next stanza. The last line of a pantoum is often the same as the first.

    The lines alternate in "Club Land" because it is a pantoum . Try your hand at a pantoum.

5. The ghazal is composed of a minimum of five couplets—and usually no more than fifteen—that are structurally, thematically, and emotionally autonomous. Each line of the poem must be of the same length, though meter is not imposed in English. The first couplet introduces a scheme, made up of a rhyme followed by a refrain. Subsequent couplets pick up the same scheme in the second line only, repeating the refrain and rhyming the second line with both lines of the first stanza. The final couplet usually includes the poet's signature, referring to the author in the first or third person, and frequently including the poet's own name or a derivation of its meaning.

    "Shoulders" is a ghazal, but not in the strictest sense of the term. There's a narrative through-line in "Shoulders" that connects the couplets, a narrative about male intimacy.
    Compose a ghazal of your own.

6. Odes are lyrical poems in the form of an address to a particular subject, often elevated in style or manner and written in varied or irregular meter.

Similar to "Ode to Godflower," write an ode to something unexpected.

7. "*Máquina de escribir lunar* (Lunar Typewriter)" is an ekphrastic poem and a concrete poem. An ekphrastic poem is a vivid description of a scene or, more commonly, a work of art. Through the imaginative act of narrating and reflecting on the "action" of a painting or sculpture, the poet may amplify and expand its meaning. A concrete poem visually matches the topic of the poem. The words form shapes which illustrate the poem's subject as a picture, as well as through literal meaning.

Write an ekphrastic poem of your own, or a concrete poem. If you can incorporate both into one piece, do so!

8. Think of a time when a moment shifted your life in another direction, to another place. List out a series of feelings and images that arise from meditating in this moment. Turn these into a poem that speaks to that moment but also the idea of movement.

ACKNOWLEDGEMENTS

Thank you to J. K. Fowler and the team at Nomadic Press for having faith in this book. An extra special thanks to James Cagney for his logical brain and indispensable wisdom.

I have deep gratitude for the mentors who helped mold this collection from its inception to the present—Karen Kevorkian, Frederick D'Aguiar, Harryette Mullen, Brian Kim Stefans, F. Douglas Brown, Clint Margrave—thank you. A big thanks to D.A. Powell for titling this collection! Many thanks to K. Soehnlein and to Ari Banias.

A shout out to the eyes, hearts and minds that helped shape these pieces, in large and small ways: Kevin Madrigal, Daniel Dias Callahan, Dylan Karlsson, Eve McNally, Anousheh Farid, Jubi Arriola-Headley, Mark Maza, and Mikey Reyes Jr.

Further thanks and warmth to A.A. Vincent, Danielle Williams, Joelle Antonio Mercedes, Delphine Candland, Jessica Powell, Hayat Hyatt, Talika Varma, Natalie Green, and Nicholas Neyhouse.

Thank you all for contributing to *Shifters*.

Many thanks to the following publications where some of these poems previously appeared in different forms:

"A Dummy's Vent," *Myriad* (2016)
"Fourth of July, Five Years," "I Carry Her Water from the Well," "Sum Daze / On a Hill," *Westwind* (2017)

RANDY JAMES

was born in Los Angeles, California in 1984. His father was a driver, and his mother, a social worker. Randy received an MFA in Writing from the University of San Francisco. He has also studied at UCLA. His work has been published in *Myriad*, *Westwind*, *Red Cedar Review, Palette,* and *FEM Newsmagazine*. Randy has performed in venues across Los Angeles and the San Francisco Bay Area. His work is featured in Hayat Hyatt's "Villanelle," which has been archived by Collectif Jeune Cinema. James currently resides in Southern California.

OTHER WAYS TO SUPPORT NOMADIC PRESS' WRITERS

In 2020, two funds geared specifically toward supporting our writers were created: the **Nomadic Press Black Writers Fund** and the **Nomadic Press Emergency Fund**.

The former is a forever fund that puts money directly into the pockets of our Black writers. The latter provides up to $200 dignity-centered emergency grants to any of our writers in need.

Please consider supporting these funds. You can also more generally support Nomadic Press by donating to our general fund via nomadicpress.org/donate and by continuing to buy our books. As always, thank you for your support!

Scan here for more information and/or to donate.
You can also donate at nomadicpress.org/store.